This Table

Meditations for the Communion Service

By Ronald G. Davis

STANDARD
PUBLISHING
Cincinnati, Ohio

Library of Congress Cataloging-in-Publication Data

Davis, Ronald G.
   This table / by Ronald G. Davis
      p. cm.
   ISBN 0-7847-0397-3
   1. Lord's Supper—Meditations.   I. Title.
   234'.163—dc20   95-821
                                              CIP

The Standard Publishing Company, Cincinnati, Ohio
A division of Standex International Corporation
© 1995 by The Standard Publishing Company
Printed in the United States of America
02 01 00 99 98 97 96 95   5 4 3 2 1

THIS TABLE

Blessed is the one who is privileged to lead a group of worshipers as they focus on the body and blood of their Lord. To remember Christ and His grand redemptive act is a central purpose of Christian worship in congregational assembly.

This collection of meditations attempts to emphasize what the Lord's table is and does. The style used is both personal and oral. Diction is oral rather than written, for these meditations are designed more to be said than read. Though they attempt to be personal, they can be further personalized by the user—and need to be in certain cases. Inserting one's own name in selected meditations or relating individual experiences appropriately will do much to make them vital and effective. For example, in a meditation such as "This Table and the Devil" (page 41), I have used *Ron* when the devil addresses the speaker; you, of course, should substitute your own name.

3

In places where *I* is used and the idea cannot accurately be used for you, such as in the reference to personal acrophobia used in "This Table, God's SeeSaw" (page 11), you may need to convert all the *I's* to third person *one's* or *a person's* . . . or choose another meditation!

The fragmented, repetitive style in these meditations requires a judicious use of oral pauses for best emphasis. Ellipses have been used to encourage a pause of longer than usual duration. Read these meditations slowly and deliberately for the full literary effect.

Each time Christians assemble around the Lord's table, the gospel is fully proclaimed. "Christ died for our sins," this table pronounces. "He is risen and one day will return," this table anticipates. Blessed are you when you so proclaim the gospel as you lead with these meditations. May all the glory and honor come to Him whom we worship at this table!

THIS TABLE
Is Set Worldwide

This table and its elements are a worldwide table. Every hour of the Lord's Day, this table is set somewhere. Five hours or more before New Yorkers do so, Christians gather in the European morning to partake. Two to five hours after Midwesterners sit reverently to recall the Calvary event, West Coasters and islanders will assemble to do so. Halfway around the world, some have partaken at a time that is for us in a different day! Since before you and I arose until after we retire for the night, Christians somewhere are stopping to remember the Lord's death and anticipate His coming again. Though time does not limit Him in Heaven, He knows the way time pushes, shoves, elbows, tugs, and harasses us. Certainly He must be pleased to see us interrupting time long enough to consider eternity.

Just think: For all the time in a day,

one-seventh of the temporal existence He created and fully understands, someone somewhere is pausing to focus on His gracious death. We are a part of that stream of remembrance. We dare not interrupt it. We dare not leave a gap in His pleasure. This is our time. This is our place. We are a vital part of a day-long reflection on Jesus' death. Just now, we are the world . . . to Him!

PRAYER: O God of eternity and Maker of time, we come in this moment to ponder how He has entered time and given us eternity. Bless all those today who give You joy in this remembrance.

Beautiful, Quiet, Calm

Most of us like those calm, quiet places outdoors where we can simply sit and enjoy the beauty, the quiet, the calm of the place. Around this table indoors, we have that same privilege.

This is a place of beauty. Here we can look up the hill thataway and see the cross silhouetted against the sky. The Son is aglow, reflecting a vermilion aura of sun against blood. Over on that other hillside yonder sits a garden . . . and a tomb, with its sealing stone rolled back. If you look carefully, you can see a glint of golden light, as it were the eternal throne of God.

This is a place of quiet. It is almost like sitting in a cemetery, behind a rural church long left empty. It is the quiet of death. And it is the quiet of awe. No words come in God's presence, for we are overwhelmed. This is a place of calm. Though Jesus knew what the night hours held for Him on that evening when He began this memorial, He brought His apostles apart into the upstairs dining room and relaxed calmly over the Passover meal and chatted casually—even if seriously—with His friends. He knew the panic that would come in the early hours of the next morning; but here, here He soothes them with His manner and His words and a song.

Enjoy this place of quiet, calm, and beauty. Soon enough we all go back to our world of noise, anxiety, and ugliness. But this, this is our special place, our retreat.

PRAYER: Thank You, Father, for this place where our souls are calm and quiet, where we see the beauty of our Savior's dying. Give us here the spirit of beauty, quiet, and calm.

THIS TABLE
Of Do's and Don'ts

Most of us do not relish lives of do's and don'ts. We think such a restricted life belongs to childhood and immaturity. And that is true. The legalistic system necessary to bring children (and young nations such as Moses' Israelites!) to maturity is appropriate and wise. Yet, though this table of our Lord is designed for the mature, those who have personally and by reason and conviction decided to join the kingdom, it is still a table of do's and don'ts.

The simple imperative, "Do this," puts every Christian under the dictum. Even though I can still choose not to participate, I cannot so choose and obey my Lord. (Of course, if I refuse to obey Him, I am denying that He is my Lord!) This table, thus, becomes a test, not of my immaturity but of my maturity. And the "don't"—"Don't act here in an unworthy manner"—forces me to look at my maturity for the day: the

9

maturity of my motives, the maturity of my commitment, the maturity of my obedience, the maturity of dealing with the "do and don't" dilemma of this table.

Sometimes do's and don'ts are for the mature. This is one of those times. This table is one of those places. *Do* this in memory of Christ; *don't* do it in an unworthy manner.

PRAYER: For the clear do's and don'ts of your Word, O God, we thank You. Help us today to test our maturity here in our obedience.

THIS TABLE
God's Seesaw

Picture this table as the giant fulcrum of an even greater seesaw.

On one end, I sit. On the other, sits God. I am unable to keep the rhythm going. In fact, I am dangling helplessly up—way up!—in the air. My goodness has the weight of a bird feather . . . a hummingbird feather. And down there—way, way down there—sits God. His righteousness is absolutely heavy; He *is* righteousness.

As long as I sit on my end by myself, I am utterly uncomfortable . . . fearful . . . it is a long way down to the abyss. And I . . . I am afraid of heights . . . panic-stricken.

Right at the moment of dread and panic, as I ponder scrambling over the edge, Christ sits down with me on my end. Ahhh . . . rhythm, grace, movement, delight. Life is fun once more.

Picture this table as the giant fulcrum

of an even greater seesaw . . . with God on one end . . . and Christ and me on the other end!

Seesaws are no fun when the two ends carry unequal weights. Seesaws don't work when the two ends carry unequal weights. But, thanks be to God, Christ has, by the cross and empty tomb, sat down on our end. He has added the weight of His righteousness to weightless shadow!

PRAYER: We come to You, heavenly Father, only because we come in the righteousness of Your own Son. Forgive our feeble efforts to keep life in balance by our own substance.

THIS TABLE
Not for Every Day

This is not an everyday table. Oh, the apostles ate with Jesus daily. Along the shore, at one of their homes, in some kind lady's kitchen, along the dusty road, in the fine home of a prominent citizen, at a well in Samaria, they ate together every day. But this table does not represent their everyday table.

This was a one-time table for them. In an upper room . . . surrounded by Jerusalem hostility. They reset this table every Lord's Day once the church established its practice of meeting and worshiping on the day of Jesus' resurrection. Every day they ate their meals, simple meals to sustain life. Every Lord's Day they ate *this* meal, a simple meal to sustain a memory of a death—Jesus' death.

Monday, Tuesday Wednesday, Thursday, Friday, Saturday we enjoy our everyday meals. They sustain us for this life. Every

Sunday we enjoy *this* meal. It gives us strength in anticipation of our life to come; for we will do this until He comes again or until we go to Him.

This is not an everyday meal. It is special. It is special in timing. It is special in purpose.

PRAYER: For this special meal, Father, we give You thanks. You know our needs for special times and places.

A Preschool Table

There is something preschoolish about this table. It is a sensory table. Preschool classrooms quite commonly have a sand and water table for play and learning. At that table, the children touch and see and hear . . . and learn. The scratchy but pleasing feel of sand dribbling through their fingers and from cupped palm to palm. The way grains of sand compress and scatter, mound and smooth. The sound of water splatting and coursing. Grains of sand precipitating a pitter-pat pattern on plastic toys and tools. The resistance of a mountain of sand to a PlaySkool bulldozer.

This table before us is a sensory table. It allows us to focus all our senses on the Lord. Here we hear the words of Jesus, "Do this in remembrance of me!" We hear the sounds of hammer blows muffled by flesh and muscle. Here we touch the bread broken. Were we preschoolers, we'd feel the bread between our fingertips . . . and remember that the Savior had fingertips at the end of impaled palms. Here we see the emblems and taste the bread and the fruit of the blood spilt. Were we four-year-olds, we'd have to hold the cup to the light and see the sparkling red. (And—unfortunately for parents and teachers—we'd probably have to pour the juice onto cloths or other surfaces to see the pool and the stain!) Here we pass the trays and reproduce the same muscle movements of the apostles who sat with Him around that table of Passover. Here the quiet calm surrounds us. Here we sense God's presence.

Can you approach this table with all the freshness, the newness of a young child? Can you step up to this sensory table with all your senses alive and ready? Are you ready to learn here?

PRAYER: Make us young here, O ageless God. Restore the freshness, the newness of this deed. Help us to learn here.

A Table of Songs

Since they accompanied Paul Simon on
his *Graceland* album, Ladysmith Black
Mambazo and their mbube singing have
been enjoyed by many. Most listeners do
not understand most of the lyrics. Though
many of the songs are gospel, they are of
South African origin and style. Scattered
throughout the songs are occasional
"Alleluias." Many musical phrases end with
a resounding "Amen!" Those two words
the listeners understand.

Celestial gospel songs resonate from
this table before us. Some of the lyrics I do
not understand. I know they are beautiful. I
know they are harmonious. Yet the ideas
are still a mystery. Occasionally here, I hear
the angelic choir in full harmony sing,
"Alleluia!" That, I recognize. Occasionally
here, I hear a sincerely inharmonious
"Amen!" That, I recognize.

For this table to have meaning and

melody, I do not need to know the meaning of the whole libretto. Theologians have interpreted the lyrics of this table for centuries. Sometimes they have erred grievously, theologian intelligence sometimes lacking common sense. But none would confuse these two words: "Alleluia!" and "Amen!" "Praise the Lord Jehovah!" and "So be it!" If you do not comprehend any of the other songs this table sings, do not fret. These two are clear and simple: "Alleluia!" "Amen!" Jesus died for my sins . . . "Alleluia!" He is coming back for me . . . "Amen!"

PRAYER: Help us, O Father of music, to hear the intricate and the plain songs of this table. We have come to say, "Alleluia!" We have come to say, "Amen!" Praise to You! Come, Lord Jesus!

Jesus Ate Here!

In many historical homes, the tour guides point—sometimes with pride and sometimes with mechanical disinterest—to the furnishings actually used by the famous person(s) who once lived there. We have all seen and heard jokes on such signs as "George Washington slept here."

Let me tell you that Jesus once reclined at this table. The apostle John was next to Him. And eleven others whose names are recorded for posterity also were there. I do not carry a mechanical disinterest in these facts. If I were a tour guide by this table, I would point with pride and great enthusiasm and say, "Jesus ate here!" And John. And eleven other apostles. Since that first occasion, millions of people, famous and not, have sat around this table, this table where Jesus ate.

Sitting and eating here does not make one famous to the world. No one will ever put up a sign, "Ron Davis Ate Here!" But sitting and eating here does make one famous to God. He knows all who sit here. He can name each one—for He knows His sheep by name (John 10:3, 14). To the angels He can boast, "My children ate here!" With deep pride and great en-thusiasm He will say, "You ate at my Son's table, didn't you?" And with corresponding pride and enthusiasm, we will be able to say, "Yes! Yes, I did."

PRAYER: For the privilege of sitting at the Son's table, Lord, we thank You. Help us here to have that godly pride and enthusi-asm appropriate to this place, this act.

THIS TABLE
Is for Guests

We sit at this table as guests. We are
here by invitation. The Host chose us to
attend, for He cared enough about us to
have us here at His table. A dinner guest
must come prepared: he cleans himself,
dresses himself appropriate to the occasion, arrives on time, greets the host,
approaches the table at the host's direction,
and sits where the host indicates.

The guest at this table comes prepared
also. We come here clean, washed clean by
the blood of our Host. We come here
dressed appropriately, in the righteous
robes woven by the grace of God. The time
arrives each Lord's Day, and we guests
have it printed in our pocket-planning
calendars; it is a regular entry. We have
greeted our Host in prayers and songs; He
has received us graciously into His house.
Now He has seated us at His table. At one
end sits the Host; He is the Head of the

table. We sit in the honored positions to His right and to His left. The food and drink are prepared and ready to be served. But first, our Host bows His holy head. He is wise enough to know that prayer is appropriate to the occasion. He knows that He is Host by the plan and intent of His Father. So He gives thanks. We know we are guests by the plan and the grace of His Father. So we also give thanks. We are guests here. We must behave properly.

PRAYER: O Heavenly Host, we sit humbly at Your table. Help us to be wise as Your guests; help us to honor the Host, Your Son. Thank You for Your gracious invitation to be present here.

Ordinary, Humdrum, Blah?

Sometimes when I approach this table, I am concerned I will let this be ordinary, humdrum, blah. Recently, a neighborhood bakery displayed a billboard: "Let us make your wedding memorable . . . with our cheesecake!" Though I am confident they did not intend to imply anything except how delicious their cheesecake is, it is possible to read that sign: "Weddings are ordinary, humdrum, blah . . . without cheesecake!" Tell a bride that. Or a groom. Weddings are essentially, intrinsically, and universally memorable. To be memorable, they do not need cheesecake, a Philharmonic orchestra, a video extravaganza, an overflowing sanctuary, several "show-stopping" musical solos, newspaper coverage, or any other "extras."

Nor does this table! It is essentially, intrinsically, and universally memorable. It cannot be ordinary, humdrum, blah. At the core it is exceptional, exciting, distinctive. What is more memorable than the grand events recalled here? What could be done—what could I do—to make it *more* memorable?

There, at that "wedding" of God's grace with my sin, the Bridegroom said, "I do!" Here, near this table, once, we came and said, "I do!" when questioned as to our belief in the lordship of Christ. What possibly could add to the memories?

PRAYER: For the wonderful memories we have at this table, God of the extraordinary, we bow to give You praise. Let us see them anew, fresh, memorable today.

Museum and Monument

In mid-April, 1993, in Washington, DC, along that golden mile of museums and government shrines, the American Holocaust Museum opened. The museum is a beautiful tribute to a ghastly deed. It remembers that millions died for one evil man. And such small places as Treblinka and Auschwitz gained a significance and infamy to last them through time.

In mid-April in the year A.D. 30 in Jerusalem, Judea, this monument—the Communion table—was opened. It is a beautiful picture of a marvelous deed. It remembers that one good Man died for millions of evil ones. And such a small place as Calvary gained a fame to last through eternity.

As ultimately horrible an event as the former was, the latter is ultimately glorious. As hidden and secretive as the former was designed to be, the latter is open and observable. As destructive and life-taking as the former was, the latter is gracious and life-giving.

Streams of visitors file through the American Holocaust Museum daily, quietly, solemnly, sadly. Here at this monument, we must also come quietly, solemnly, sadly. Stand silently and reverently here . . . for Jesus has died, for the sins of all.

PRAYER: For the One who died for the many, we come to praise You, O God. Let this table remind us of the absolute terror and horror of sin in the world. Help us, Father, to so hate sin that we will speak of righteousness at every opportunity.

THIS TABLE
of the Friend

In old Jerusalem there is a gate that
allows access through the medieval city
wall. The Arabs call it simply, "The Gate of
the Friend." The gate honors Abraham, the
"friend of God."

Here, we have a table that allows access
through the barrier wall of sin. We could
well call it, "The Table of the Friend." Jesus
said, in that intensely personal dialogue He
shared with His apostles in John 14–17, "I
no longer call you servants . . . I have
called you friends" (John 15:15). "You are
my friends if you do what I command"
(15:14). We thus have every right to call
this "The Table of the Friend, *Our* Friend,"
for here we do what the Friend commands.
Sometimes in everyday life and relation-
ships, one will do what a friend says and it
ends up disastrously. But a part of friend-
ship is trusting the judgment of another.
We have never done anything the Friend—

capitol *F*—has directed, and found disaster. When we do what the Friend says, we find joy, delight, peace.

Welcome to "The Table of the Friend." Confidently and expectantly, do what He says to do. He is your Friend! Doing this, we will be honoring our Friend. Doing this, we will be honored by our Friend.

PRAYER: O Friend of friends, we come to do what You have commanded. Thank You for taking away our servitude to sin and making us Your friends.

THIS TABLE
An Inscribed Table

This is an inscribed table. A craftsman with proper tools and expert skill cut the words, "This Do in Remembrance of Me." Schoolteachers know inscribed tables. Idle and thoughtless students with the wrong tools and amateurish ability cut words such as, "Euberta Loves Odell," or simply a hideous stick-figure caricature with the caption, "T-E-E-C-H-U-R!" But even those crude inscriptions bespeak deep emotion and sentiment. Euberta *did* love Odell—at least for a day. And the teacher had so bruised a student's spirit, the student had to react—even if in the partially concealed manner of desktop graffiti.

The inscription on our table here must also incite and reflect deep emotion and sentiment—and not in a transitory mental doodle. These words cut here across the front of the table were carefully planned and painstakingly carved. With concentration and intense thought, the words have been inscribed there. Our attention to the events for which the words exist must be carefully planned, painstakingly rendered; with concentration and intense thought, we will "do this in remembrance of" Christ. He is the Word inscribed on our hearts.

PRAYER: Inscribe our hearts, Lord, with the words of His grace. Put the word of redemption on our foreheads. Help us to so reflect the Word of Christ that all will see Him written in our lives.

THIS TABLE
An Every-Week Table

Some Christians do not understand why we meet around this table every week. Of course, Jesus' directive was simply, *as often* as you do this, do it in remembrance of me (1 Corinthians 11:25). The New Testament church's practice appears to have been "on the first day of the week" they gathered "to break the bread" (Acts 20:7). Such apostolic precedent, at the leadership of the ones present in that upper room of origin, has the stamp of approval of inspired men. Christians who do not understand our practice opine, "Doesn't it get old and meaningless?" (Some of those same Christians pray the Lord's model prayer *every* Sunday . . . but I won't ask about that getting old and meaningless.) Well, my answer is, "It *is* old . . . 1,970 years worth of old!" It does not "get" old. And I do not have to give meaning to it. It *has* intrinsic meaning. If I am so dull of spiritual senses that it *seems* meaningless, I need to consider myself and partake of it *more* than others do, not less frequently.

Every week was just right for first-century Christians. Every week is just right for me.

PRAYER: Thank You, God of order, for making this table weekly. Let us live by Your Spirit from Sunday to Sunday in its anticipation. Remind us of its age and of its meaning.

A Song of Anguish at

In 2 Samuel 1:19-27, David sang a song of anguish over the deaths of Saul, his King, and Jonathan, his friend. Here, at this table, we sing a song of anguish . . . at the death of our Friend and King. David's words, with a few adaptations, are a worthy song to be sung at this table:

The beauty of Israel is slain on the high place;
How the Mighty has fallen!
Do not tell it in the place of death;
Let it not be told in the dark places of Hades,
Lest those children of darkness delight,
Lest those fallen ones think "victory."
O mountain of Jerusalem,
Let there be no daytime light,
Nor let there be the rain of gladness,
Nor growing things of value;
For the shield of the Mighty is defiled,
The shield of Jesus, as if He were not

the Anointed of God!
O children of the kingdom, weep over
    Joshua,
Who has given us His clothes of right-
    eousness,
Who has decorated us with His Spirit!
How the Mighty has fallen;
At the climax of the battle between good
    and evil;
The Friend was slain in this high place.

O I am distressed for You,
My Brother, Christ the Lord;
You have been my salvation;
Your love to me is wonderful,
Surpassing all the love of men.
How the Mighty has fallen!

PRAYER: We come to You with anguished
hearts, God of Israel, for our Mighty One
has fallen in death . . . on our behalf . . . for
our sins. Let not the devil rejoice. Let him
and his cohorts see the glory of the resur-
rected Lord. Take our grief and make it the
joy of life in Jesus.

THIS TABLE
Is Two-Sided

This is a two-sided table. Though often we have pushed this table up against something, it is two-sided. If we sit to one side, we see in full profile the Lord as fully human. Capable of emotion and pain. Capable of sin and good works. From our view, we can see—He has eye, ear, nose, mouth, arm, body. He has flesh. Capable of bleeding and of death.

If we sit to the other side, we see in full profile the Lord as fully divine. Capable of absolute knowledge and absolute power. Capable of resisting sin. Capable of forgiving sin—even of those who drove nails into His body and even of those who demanded it. Capable of defeating death by resurrection!

This is a two-sided table. We need to sit on both sides viewing Jesus, born of Mary and eternally preexistent; Jesus, Son of God and child of Nazareth and Jerusalem.

King of kings and foot-washer supreme. Christ of Old Testament prophecy and carpenter's apprentice.

Sit on both sides of the table today. Eat with your Friend. Eat with the Lord of the universe.

PRAYER: Humble us, God of gods, by our awareness of the deity of our Lord Jesus. Lift us, Father of our brother Jesus, by our sensitivity to Your nearness to us in Him.

THIS TABLE
Is for Sinners

Jesus never hesitated to sit down to eat with sinners. At Matthew's house (Luke 5:29-31), His habit to do so brought the accusatory remarks of the Pharisees and law teachers. But, of course, they timidly leveled the indictments against His disciples, not at Him directly: "Why do *you* eat and drink with tax collectors and 'sinners'?" Yet, Jesus, of course, jumped in to answer . . . a simple answer: "It is not the healthy who need a doctor, but the sick. I have not come to call the righteous, but sinners to repentance."

At this table, Jesus risks the same accusation. For here He sits down to eat with "tax collectors and sinners." It does not matter if one is a specialist sinner, a "tax collector," or a generalist sinner—Jesus does not hesitate to pull up a seat and sit here.

What sins do you bring to the table?

Never fear—"The blood of Jesus . . . purifies us from every sin" (1 John 1:7)! He sits down beside us, sin or not. His presence here at this table does not make Him a sinner. It makes Him a Savior. It does not in any way degrade or humiliate Him. In every way, it elevates and honors us. His righteousness "rubs off" on ourselves here.

Jesus never hesitates to sit down and eat with sinners. And aren't you glad? I am!

PRAYER: We come fearfully into Your presence, holy God, for we are sinners. Yet we come joyfully because Your Son has sat down with us. Forgive our sins.

Is a Worship Table

Our worship at this table has three essential elements of worship: seeing God for who He is, seeing ourselves for what we are, and responding to the great difference between Him and us.

Here we stop to see and honor God for who He is: Father of our Lord Jesus Christ, designer of our salvation. At Calvary, we have our best picture of Him, a picture of holiness, love, and grace.

Here we see ourselves for what we are: sinners whose sins are so great the God of Creation had to redeem us with the blood of His only begotten Son. Here we see ourselves for what we are: inadequate . . . inadequate to save ourselves, inadequate even to remember on our own the death of the Lord Jesus, without this table of remembrance.

Here we respond to the vast difference between God's power and holiness and our weakness and sinfulness. We submit to His lordship; we obey His command, "Do this!" We admit our sins to Him and ask for *His* continuing patience and forgiveness.

Here, at this table, we worship. We see God. We see ourselves. We cry out, "Help!"

PRAYER: Accept our worship in this act, O God. May we see You fully. May we see our own sins in their darkness. We worship Your holiness; we repent of our sins.

And the Devil

The devil sits at this table. He has found a seat cozied up to some of us here. Even if we try to spread our Bible and our hymnal out to leave no room beside us, he is not polite. He pushes them up against us, grins, and says, "No one sitting here, is there, friend?" He does not belong here, but neither did he belong on the mountain with Jesus. Jesus, who had fasted week after week, as He pondered His ministry of redemption in full worship of His Father, did not want or need the devil there. But there he was, full of lies and jeers.

"Think about yourself, Jesus. If God is Your Father, He would not leave You out here hungry. Think about yourself, Jesus. Even these stones look good enough to eat, don't they? Think about yourself, Jesus. There are quicker ways to fame and recognition. Jump, Jesus, Jump—from here to temple to courtyard, Jesus. What a splash! Think about me, Jesus . . . and what I can give you . . . whole kingdoms of blindly loyal followers. Think about anything, Jesus, anything but servanthood and dying."

And the devil sits here, sometimes right up next to me, comfortably uncomfortable next to me . . . whispering in my ear, "Think about yourself, Ron." And he is persistent and clever. But I—and you—must do as Jesus did. With the full authority of the Word, we turn and call loudly in his face, "Be gone! Be gone with thoughts of food and fame and power and glory. Be gone!"

The devil is faithful to come here every Lord's Day, even though he does not belong here. You and I belong here. We belong here . . . with thoughts of servanthood, of dying, of Jesus.

PRAYER: For the power of the indwelling Word, we pray, O Lord. For the power to resist the thoughts the devil would have us think. Give us thoughts of service, of dying, of Jesus our Lord.

Is for Seeing and Sorting

Tables are where we spread things out to see and to sort. From dress patterns and cloth for sewing preparation to last year's receipts for income tax form preparation.

This table of the Lord is a seeing and sorting table. Here is spread out the emblems of the Lord's death. We see them and they enable us to sort out meanings and values.

In His death, we see sins: their sins, our sins, her sins, his sins . . . my sins. In a single pile, they have caused God's grace and compassion to act . . . for "without the shedding of blood there is no forgiveness" of sins (Hebrews 9:22). In separate, individual, personal piles—large or small—they are weighty enough to kill each of us . . . "for the wages of sin is death" (Romans 6:23). But God has swept all the piles together and then swept them all off the table. And He has cast them as far away as

His power allows. And He is omnipotent!

On this table, we begin to understand values. "What good will it be for a man if he gains the whole world, yet forfeits his soul?" (Matthew 16:25). Soul is more valuable than things. What we see at this table helps us sort out ultimate values. For God so valued the world, He was willing to allow His own Son to die as the price for that valuable thing He had created: men's souls!

Make this your seeing and sorting table today. See Christ's righteousness and your own sinfulness. But let what you see sort out what God values and what we must value: souls—our own and those of others. See and sort. See and sort.

PRAYER: We have come here, O Lord, to see what You have done in Christ. We have come to see what You value. Give us the vision to see, the wisdom to value as You value.

THIS TABLE
Placement

Where does this table and the partaking of its emblems fit chronologically in a worship service?

At the beginning? This act does stimulate the thoughts that are to be primary in our worship: that God allowed His only Son to die for our sins to redeem us to himself. What more appropriate thought to begin a service?

In the middle of the service? This act of submitting to the lordship of our Christ and obeying His directives is at the very core of our worship. So, at the core of the hour seems most fitting.

At the end of the service? One last collective affirmation that we believe all the truths that have been read, sung, and spoken would be an apt conclusion.

Of course, the placement of the Lord's Supper within the worship service is *not* the significant question. It will "fit" anywhere. Beginning, middle, or end. The significant questions are: Does it stimulate the relevant thought? Does it reflect submission and obedience? Does it truly affirm my belief . . . and yours? Concern yourself not with when it is done . . . only in what spirit and manner it is done.

PRAYER: Forgive us, Father, when we dwell on minor elements in our worship. By Your Spirit, allow us to focus on the death of Christ and its meaning to us.

THIS TABLE
Feels Like Home

Meeting around this table is like coming home. One is always welcome . . . at home. At home, things and events are where and how you expect to find them; they're dependable. The family gathers . . . at home. Home provides a certain feeling of safety and peace—if it's a good home. Home is where most find nurture and rest. At home, you can be yourself—no pretensions; of course, they would not fool anyone there! No businesslike demeanor must be carried home; that can be left at the workplace.

So here, at this table, we have come home. We are welcomed by the Head of the house, the kindest Father. We have come to a dependable table; it is always here, ready for us. The whole family gathers here . . . in harmony and comfort. Here we enjoy our soul's safety and our spirit's peace, leaving the hectic and annoying "out there" out there! Here we can be ourselves—we must be ourselves. None of our spiritual pretensions will come close to deceiving our Father. We are here fully open to His omniscient eye. But there is no intimidation or fear here, for He is grace and love and compassion. This table is not business; it is pleasure.

Here the welcome mat is laid. Here the Father opens the door, and with a broad smile, He says, "WELCOME HOME!"

PRAYER: We come as loving children to our loving Father to say, "Thank You, Father, for a home of quiet, calm, and comfort. We are pleased by Your open door in Christ Jesus. Help us to feel at home here."

Our "Mindstring"

Though I am not sure I have ever seen anyone wearing a string around a finger as a reminder to do some important task, I have seen many prompting devices at work: magnet-attached notes on refrigerators; Post-It notes stuck on typewriters, mirrors, and dashboards; coded computer messages that pop up on the screen at relevant times; even page after page of Day-Timer memos. It is quite human to forget. We get so occupied with one task that we become oblivious to another pressing one.

God—who knows yesterday, today, and tomorrow—created man with only limited abilities to know and remember. So He created this table as our "mindstring" to remind us of the death of His Son each time we assemble. As one for whom the details of yesterdays are predictably fading, I appreciate God's prompting device. I am glad He has posted a note here in front of us: "Do this in remembrance of me." I am glad the memo is written there in our bulletin: "Communion." I am glad He has set this table here in this conspicuous place. I need this table. It helps me remember, even when my thoughts are occupied with a thousand and one lesser tasks. When I seem to be oblivious to the greater, pressing task of obeying my Lord, He gives this table, my "mindstring." I need this table. It helps me remember.

PRAYER: Lord, You provide our every need in Christ Jesus. We come to honor You as the giver of every good and perfect gift. For this remembering device, we thank You. For the memories it stirs, we praise You.

THIS TABLE
Is Not for Everyone

This is not a table for everyone. For some there is absolutely no meaning to it. For one "walking in off the street" with absolutely no knowledge of Christ's death and its purpose, this table is nothing. For one who knows superficially of a person named Jesus who did something, somewhere, sometime, this table is nothing. For someone who has a working knowledge of Jesus, with a few brain-held details of His birth, life, and death, but no concept of His deity and His redemptive work, this table is nothing. For anyone who has not believed that Jesus is the Christ of God and who has not made Him Savior and Lord, this table is nothing. This is not a table for everyone.

But, for those of us who know Christ's death and its purpose; for those of us who know He submitted to a cruel death on Calvary in the time of the Roman Empire in A.D. 30; for those of us who know intimate details of Bethlehem, Nazareth, Jerusalem; for those of us who have believed that Jesus is the Christ of God and who have made Him both Savior and Lord; for us . . . this table is everything.

PRAYER: By Your grace and by the testimony of others, O God, we have come to know Jesus as Lord and Savior. Thank You for those who told us. Thank You for making this table means so much for us by allowing Your Son to die for our sins.

Is a Celebration

The word *celebrate* is in revival for worship services. Indeed, some congregations call their whole gathering a "celebration." *Celebrate* is from a Latin participle meaning "to frequent, go in great numbers, to honor." *Webster's New World Dictionary* (Third College Edition) gives the word its meanings in essentially historical order: (1) "to perform (a ritual or ceremony) publicly and formally"; (2) "to commemorate with ceremony or festivity"; (3) "to honor or praise publicly"; (4) "to mark (a happy occasion) by engaging in some pleasurable activity." So when the Roman Catholic Church speaks of "celebrating Mass," it is using the term appropriately for the Lord's Supper.

There is ritual at this table. Oh, not some mechanical performance of meaningless acts. But there is solemn formality here. There is procedure here.

There is commemoration here. We come with memories. It is those memories that bind us here. We commemorate Christ's death on our behalf.

There is honor and praise here—honor to the most honorable Lord of the universe; honor to the suffering servant Jesus Christ. Praise fills the air here, praise for the deed done . . . and for the Doer of the deed.

There is happiness here, for this is a pleasurable activity.

We have great reason to be happy here, for sins are gone and sinners are saved!

Ritual. Commemoration. Honor. Praise. Happiness. Pleasure. This table is a celebration . . . by anyone's definition.

PRAYER: We come to celebrate Your grace, O God. Accept our ritual here, for it is done with emotion and sincerity. Accept the honor and the praise we bring. Give us happiness and pleasure here.

THIS TABLE
Is Confusing

This can be a confusing table. Imagine the puzzlement of those in Capernaum who heard the first hints of this table. Jesus said, "I tell you the truth, unless you eat the flesh of the Son of Man and drink his blood, you have no life in you. Whoever eats my flesh and drinks my blood has eternal life . . . for my flesh is real food and my blood is real drink" (John 6:53-55). Jesus' lesson on that occasion had begun with mild condemnation of His listeners for seeking Him for another free lunch of fish and bread. But then He took an abrupt turn to a spiritual homily concerning symbols and eternal substance. And His listeners grumbled, "This is too hard!"

This *is* a hard table. Jesus' body? Jesus' blood? Does anyone understand it? Is everyone confused?

We can respond the same way many did at Capernaum: walk away shaking our heads and mumbling, "This is just too hard for me. I want something easier to understand. I'll look for another messiah." Or we can respond with Peter, "Lord, to whom shall we go? You have the words of eternal life. We believe and know that you are the Holy One of God" (vv. 68, 69).

This is a hard table. We do not come because we fully understand all the symbol or all the substance of it. We come because we believe. We come because we know that Jesus, the bread of life, is the Holy One of God.

PRAYER: Help our feeble minds to understand what we do here, O wise Father. We do believe; help our unbelief. Forgive us when we consider this table too hard; forgive us when we consider it too easy.

THIS TABLE
Is Not Empty

This is not an empty table. At many churches up and down the road this morning, the Lord's table is empty. Well, not actually empty, for someone has probably decorated it beautifully with a large flower arrangement, a large open Bible, two golden candlesticks, or some such ornamentation. But the table *is* empty, empty of the elements it was designed to hold.

Here at our church, whenever we assemble on the Lord's Day, this table is not empty. We always find it set, set with the trays of the unleavened bread representing the Lord's body, and with trays of pure fruit of the vine to symbolize our Lord's blood.

Know that on the Lord's Day this table will not be empty of the emblems it is designed to hold . . . until the Lord comes. Know that this table will not be empty of memories . . . until the Lord makes memory of His grand redemptive deed of the past into the reality of His grand redemptive deed of His coming again. Then these emblems and these memories will slip into the shadow of times past, even as time itself slips into the shadow of eternity.

The Lord has not left this table empty. Our worship planners have not left this table empty. We dare not make it empty by our indifference, our lack of spiritual sensitivity. It is a full table, full of meaning, full of memory, full of reality.

PRAYER: For the fullness of this table, O God of fullness, we express our thanksgiving. Never let us empty it of its emblems, its meaning, its value.

THIS TABLE
Is a Worktable

This table is a worktable. Many of you have a worktable at home, whether in the garage or tool shed, the kitchen, the basement, or the bedroom. It is the table where you fashion with your hands works of art and utility.

This is God's worktable. What God has fashioned here is also a work of art and of utility. The deed represented here has been the subject of the world's best-known verbal and visual artists. From the *Pietà* of Michelangelo to "The Old Rugged Cross" of George Bennard, this table and its essence have stirred the minds and talents of many.

But this worktable has also produced the most useful product ever conceived: forgiveness. And it is a non commercial product; it is not sold—it is given away. In the same manner that many of you create delightful objects on your worktables and *give* them away, God here produced the most costly free thing imaginable: redemption! With His own mind and with His own hands, He fashioned a plan and its fulfillment. As divine potter, He shaped a magnificent Lamb, put it in a crucible of death, and displayed it fully alive from a garden tomb.

Here we have come to admire and enjoy the beauty and the utility of this table, this worktable. We have sung the beautiful words and prayed them. We have envisioned the lovely images of Bethlehem, Galilee, and Jerusalem. We have come to appreciate the usefulness of this table's meaning to our souls. It is God's worktable.

PRAYER: For the beauty and the usefulness of Your worktable we have come to honor You, great Worker of our redemption. For the image of outstretched, nail-pierced hands, we humbly praise You.

THIS TABLE
Is a Study Table

Students and scholars spend a good deal of their time at library study tables, poring over the wisdom—and the foolishness—of men. The Lord's table is a study table. Here we consider the wisdom of God. To some, of course, His wisdom—sacrificing His Son—is foolishness. But, as Paul says, "The foolishness of God is wiser than man's wisdom" (1 Corinthians 1:25).

Are you ready for this study table? Do you have your pen and paper at hand? Can you, in both broad and fine strokes, delineate the wisdom of God here? Does it sometimes seem like so much foolishness? Are you making this table your study table?

Study tables raise questions. They create wrinkled brows and head-scratching. But study tables also answer questions and create "aha's!" and "Yes-s-s's!" There is both a struggle and a victory at a study table. A struggle with truth. A struggle

with self. A struggle, here, with God himself—as it were, wrestling with an angel.
Yet the victory is here as well. The victory
of conclusions drawn. Decisions made. Self
conquered.

Today, make this table your study table.
Consider both the wisdom and the foolishness of God. Contrast that with your own
wisdom and foolishness. With that contrast
in mind, you *will* worship . . . you will worship at this study table.

PRAYER: God of wisdom, You know our
own wisdom would keep us away from this
study table. We thank You for revealing
Your wisdom in the person of Christ. Help
us to be wise.

A Place to Relax

Tables are usually places to relax. Except when dining at five-star restaurants, which creates a bit of rigidity and unease for most of us who do not frequent them, sitting at a table is generally a time of informality and ease.

Such is God's intention for us here at Christ's table. We should feel no rigidity or discomfort here. Respect is appropriate. Quiet is fitting. Yet, here we should not be tense, emotionally restrained, or struggling with personal inadequacies. No one sits here because of personal adequacy. We all approach this table *because* we have been deemed adequate by the gift and grace of the Lord. No tension should arise within us here. We can sit comfortably here, relaxed—*ahhh!*—because our sins are forgiven, because the unbearable burden on our soul's shoulders has been lifted and carried away! This is no place to restrain our emotions, no hushed whispers of the French Gourmet Room. Emotions well up in crescendo here: grief for the death of our Friend, elation for a gift given. Though we may express those emotions privately and toward God, there can be no restraining them.

This is a table where we can relax, for we have been loosed from our sins! Sit back. Relax. Enjoy.

PRAYER: Give us the sighs of release and relief, great Burden-bearer. Loose us from the bonds of guilt even as You have loosed us from the bonds of sin. Thank You for this table of relaxation.

THIS TABLE
Is a Peace Table

By the Spirit, Paul wrote to the Colossians, "For God was pleased . . . through him [Jesus] to reconcile to himself all things, . . . by making peace through his blood, shed on the cross" (Colossians 1:19, 20).

Many great military confrontations ended at a peace table: in a farmhouse at Appomattox Courthouse, on the deck of the *SS Missouri,* at a renaissance palace at the edge of Paris. On those tables ended the American Civil War, World War II, and the Vietnam War.

So it is true here: The great war for the human soul ends at this peace table; Jesus has made peace by the blood of His cross. The treaty between God and man was signed in His blood. The terms of peace are written here. The extent of the peace is defined here. It is finished, the Peacemaker declared, the war is over. Though skirmishes persist for those who have not received news of the peace, the war is over! Though the defeated one—to boost his damaged, destroyed pride—persists, the war is over.

This is our peace table. We have not come as victors, but as defeated ones, defeated by sin and death. But the Victor is gracious and forgiving. Here we surrender, but we surrender into the hands of One we know wants the best for us, One who loves us . . . in spite of the warfare we long waged against Him. This is our peace table.

PRAYER: We surrender to You here, O Victor of our souls. We have come to announce to You that we no longer wage war against Your kingdom. Forgive us for past battles; make us one of Your soldiers of the cross.

Of Memories and Experience

Memories are based on experience, so
when Jesus says, "Do this to remember
me," He assumes we have experiences with
Him. What memories come to mind for
you? Did your grandmother have one of
these garishly scary pictures of Jesus with
His heart on the outside of His body . . .
dripping blood? Can you remember back to
the day you were robed in a too-long white
robe and led up the steep, steep steps to
the baptistery pool? Or down a slippery
bank to the cold waters of a nearby stream?
Do you recall the first time a devoted
Sunday school teacher or evangelist read or
described the crucifixion in its horrid
details? What memories come to you here?
What experiences with Jesus dominate
your mind as we assemble today? Our
memories are based on our experiences
and on His. This is the table to remember
experiences—His on behalf of us, and ours

in relationship to Him. He died on our behalf for our sins. We, in baptism, died to sin. Those are the experiences we must remember here: His death *and* our own.

All the other images that come to mind—pictures we've seen and words we have heard—may be important to our thinking, but only two facts are essential: Christ died for our sins; we have died to sin in Him.

PRAYER: We have come to focus, O Lord, on death and dying. Repaint for us those sad pictures of Your Son, dying on a cruel cross. Brighten the glad colors of our impressions of the day each of us died to sin in the watery grave of baptism.

THIS TABLE
Is for Focus Groups

Businesses today often use focus groups to evaluate their effectiveness and plan their futures. Leaders settle around tables to discuss goals, strategies, successes, failures. There is a look at the past—to judge quality of procedure; there is a look to the future—to plot initiatives and methodology.

Here, at this table, we become a "focus group." Here we must focus on personal effectiveness; we must examine ourselves . . . how are we doing? We must assign grades and ratings to ourselves. Do I get an *A, B, C, D* on prayer life? Do I get an *A, B, C, D* on kindness? Here we must focus on the future, for we do this until He comes. We must make plans here—plans for improvement. When can I take time for more prayer? Who needs my kindness and how will I show it?

There is both evaluation and planning

here. We focus on Him; we want to see ourselves standing by Him . . . with the inevitable contrast that quickly highlights our own inadequacies and His all-sufficiency. Here we focus on Him: He is victorious Lord, seated in power in Heaven, but coming again—one last time—to establish His ultimate and eternal lordship over all. Focus. Focus. Focus on the past and the future. Let nothing distract you. Focus.

PRAYER: For this focus table, we thank You, God, for the past and the future. Allow us to see our strengths and our weaknesses, even as we see that He is omnipotent—that His weakness is stronger than our strength.

THIS TABLE
Can Be Extended

Many homes have one of those fine dining-room tables that can be extended and retracted. Two more for dinner? No problem. Put in another leaf. Sometimes only two people will sit down at one of those tables for a meal. Other times, twelve or more will be seated there. The table becomes whatever size is needed.

So, too, for this table before us. On Sunday evening, only a few come to this table. At some churches, there may be only two or three. On Sunday morning at those same churches, hundreds may assemble. No matter the size of the crowd who come to satisfy their spiritual hunger, God provides. Worldwide, millions come. And no one is turned away for lack of space or provision. To paraphrase the words of Ira F. Stanphill,

There is room at this table for me;
There is room at this table for me;

Tho' millions may come, there's still
  room for one;
Yes, there is room at the table for me.
  Should another and another come—
and another—the Father simply turns to
the Son and says, "Help Me add another
leaf, my Son." And the Son is *pleased* to do
so. This table is big enough for all to come.
There is body and blood here for all who
desire it, for Christ is big enough and gracious enough.

PRAYER: Thank You, O great Host, for the
open invitation to Your table. Thank You
for the invitation bearing my name. Help
us today to sense the size of this table and
the size of the deed it represents.

THIS TABLE
Is Real and More Real

This table is real wood. All the elements on it are real: real cloth, real metal trays, real wafers, real juice. Yet, there is a greater reality here . . . a spiritual reality more real than the material things here.

These things all represent the handiwork and processes of men. A logger and a carpenter made the table. A miner and a machine-tool specialist prepared the implements. A harvester, miller, and baker made the loaf. A vine grower and juice processor are responsible for the juice.

But there is a greater handiwork here, the handiwork of God himself. He took the raw materials of life itself: sin, grace, forgiveness—and fashioned those realities into a cross . . . a real cross . . . a real cross that became real redemption. Ah, there's the spiritual reality of this real table. "Redeemed—how I love to proclaim it!" Fanny Crosby affirmed. Redeemed . . . here we proclaim its reality.

That redemption, that forgiveness, is as real—no, more real—than the wood, cloth, metal, vegetable matter, liquid we use here to acknowledge that Christ really lived, really died, really arose, really sits on His throne in Heaven by the right hand of His Father. That is real, indeed!

PRAYER: Our minds are small, infinite God. To comprehend the reality of Christ's death and our forgiveness is hard for us. But You are our Creator; You know our weakness. Help us to see the reality beyond our fleshly senses.

His Guests at

THIS TABLE

Jesus often sat at peoples' tables as their guest. Some of His hosts were friends. Some were actually hostile to His purposes. At Matthew's house, Jesus joined a businessmen's dinner, sitting among those with whom Matthew worked. At the home of Lazarus, Mary and Martha treated Him like a cherished family member. At the house of Zaccheus, the Guest made the host humble by the service of His words. Jesus, at anyone's table, was an ideal guest. He did not come with demands for fine food or the seat of honor. He brought vibrant conversation. He enjoyed the company and the occasion. When He left the table, hosts were glad He had been present.

We have come to Jesus' table as His guests. Our host is our Friend, and we are fully sympathetic to His purposes. Here, we sit among those with whom He works. He treats us lovingly, as His family members.

And we want to be, at His table, ideal guests.

Here we make no demands; we accept graciously what He gives to us. We have come with the lively conversation of our prayers. We take joy in the company of believers and at the occasion of His redemptive death. When we leave His table behind, we want our Host to be glad we were present. We want our own gladness to be evident to all. We come as His guests. We leave as His servants.

PRAYER: Heavenly Host, we thank You for the invitation to sit at Your table. For the joyous fellowship here, we give You our praise. Help us, by Your Spirit, to be ideal guests.

THIS TABLE
Is a Mystery

All of us have seen the intriguing way television mystery shows are often introduced. The camera pans slowly across table tops, zooming in on a variety of items—photographs, personal grooming items, matchboxes, perhaps a gun—but the viewer does not even know what the crime is yet. It is a mystery.

Panning across this table before us, the camera would capture plates filled with broken pieces of bread and circles of cups, filled with a reddish liquid. Quite a mystery. Only this time the viewer knows what crimes have been committed . . . because each viewer is the perpetrator. The blood stains noticed are real ones; Someone has died. Was it murder? And these elements seen here on the table—what do they have to do with the treacherous events of this story? What do they mean? It is a mystery.

Now, if one has seen the TV show

before, the mystery is gone. The viewer knows both the crime and the consequences. You and I have seen this table before, perhaps hundreds or thousands of times. We know both the crime of the cross and the crimes of our lives. We know that the cross was the consequence for Jesus. We know that eternity apart from God is the consequence of our crimes . . . if they were not forgiven.

But, ah, there's the continuing mystery of this table: Christ died for the ungodly. The consequences of our crimes have been given to Another! Though we may find the story of this table very familiar, may we never allow it to lose its mystery. Who can comprehend it? Who could have ever solved it? Only God. It is His mystery.

PRAYER: For doing what we never could have conceived or resolved, we praise You, O God. For the mystery of Christ and His death, we thank You.

THIS TABLE
Is a Catafalque

This table is a catafalque (*ka*-ta-faulk). In a funeral home, at the front of the room sits the catafalque, the table-like furnishing on which the casket and its dead body is presented for loved ones to come, to express their grief, to express their love.

It does not matter what comments are made—"My, doesn't he look so natural?"; "She is so peaceful looking"—the fact is, the person is dead.

Here, at the front of this room, sits a table, on which a dead body is on display. Christ said it clearly, "This is my body . . . this is my blood." And we are His loved ones, come to express our grief, come to express our love. Yet we cannot make the comments: "He looks so natural here!" or "My, how peaceful He looks!" Death is far from natural for Him; He is Lord of life! He *is* Life! He was never at peace in death. In His death He was not at peace, but at war!

Nothing was more unnatural for Him than to die; He is everlasting, without beginning or end. Nothing close to peace filled Him. Gethsemane was agony. Calvary was convulsive torment.

What can we say of Him here? Here at this catafalque, we must say, "My, how lovely He is . . . for He . . . He is our Lord of life. He is our peace!"

PRAYER: Here we are grieved, Lord, because we view Your dead body, dead because of our actions, not Your own. We have come in love, to honor Your memory. But we come also in the gladness of our faith that You are alive.

THIS TABLE
Is for Doing

This is a table for doing. Jesus made it an imperative: "This *do* in remembrance of me." Though we often think of this as a table for thinking, pondering, meditating, praying—and it is!—it *is* a table for doing.

External, overt action occurs here. We pass and share the emblems, as a token of our community. We select and touch emblems of flesh and blood, for we have flesh and blood. We are common with Him, for He became flesh and blood to be common with us. Here we chew and sip and swallow; we consume for we want consummation with Him.

Internal, covert action occurs here as well. We create mental images of His passion. We do not "hide" these images from others; it is simply that they are *our* images—our foot-of-the-cross view—and they are personal. Here we praise Him silently for dying for us. It is not that His praise must be kept quiet, but again, this is personal: It is my praise to Him, and yours is yours. Here we repent in His presence—not that our repentance cannot be public; but once again, repentance is intensely personal and emotional. We would not want to risk it becoming a public show of false humility.

There is a sense of passivity here. For our sins, we had to wait for the Lord to act. And here we are waiting on the Lord . . . this is His table. But we must act here. There must be activity here—physical, mental, emotional, spiritual activity. For this is a table for doing. *Do* this in remembrance of Christ!

PRAYER: Accept our prayer, O great Worker of redemption. You have done on our behalf and now we do on behalf of Your Son. Make our motives pure; make our deeds honorable.

THIS TABLE
Is the Focal Point

This table is at a focal point in our worship space. It sits front and center. On occasions, when it is moved—for weddings, dramas, choral events—its absence is noticed. I always look for it. Our time focused on the emblems it holds is a focal point in our worship experience. Should the occasion arrive when it is moved or omitted, its absence would be conspicuous. I would definitely look for it.

The intensity focused on the Savior whose death this table symbolizes is the focal point of our gathering. Do I have the same "something's missing" feeling when my focal intensity on Him is lacking? How far, how deeply, would I look for it?

There is nothing wrong with moving this table on special occasions that necessitate it. Nothing wrong with moving the event to a different time within our service. But *every* thing is wrong when He is misplaced or missing in my thoughts. He must be the focal point.

Photographers plan their images very carefully, making certain the object that is the essence of their picture is in a position where the eyes of a viewer will easily find it and where the eyes are likely to linger, to focus. They call that spot the focal point. At this table, we want to plan our images very carefully, making certain He who is the essence of our picture is right there . . . right there in the focal point.

PRAYER: By Your Spirit, O God, give us focus here. Make the images sharp and plain. Let us see Christ dying willfully on the cross. Let us hear His words, "Father, forgive them . . . ."

Raises Questions

This table raises questions. What are yours? Some of mine are simple, some are not. What role has my sin played in Jesus' death? Exactly which of the thorns, the lashes, the nails were given because of me? (That one's simple: all of them, of course!) How could the Father forsake the Son . . . His only begotten Son? (That one's tough: even Jesus raised that question.) How could those Jewish scholars be so dense? They were scholars, devoted to God's Word. Why could they not comprehend the basic concept of a suffering servant? How could those people in Jerusalem have been so wishy-washy . . . raising palm leaves one day—leaves that called just ahead of the rocks, "Hosanna! Hosanna!"—and raising angry voices another day, voices calling from the abyss of Hell itself: "Crucify! Crucify!"? And that question always scares me a bit, for it always elicits another: What if I had been a Jerusalemite there and then? How could God forgive my sin and all the sins of all people of all times by having His Son die? I'm not sure I have that answer either, but I'm glad God confirmed it: "The blood of Jesus, his Son, purifies us from every sin" (1 John 1:7).

This table raises questions. Hard questions. Answerable and unanswerable questions. Questions of life . . . and of death. Questions of time . . . and eternity. What are your questions as we gather here? What are your answers?

PRAYER: We approach You in our ignorance, God of wisdom. We cannot come in pride or self-satisfaction, for we are weak of mind, and ignorant of so much truth that is here. Give us wisdom, O God. Answer our questions in this table.

THIS TABLE
Is a Unity Table

This table is a unity table, yet it has often separated brothers and sisters in the church, past *and* present. This is a unity table, yet occasionally some would build a partition across the table . . . or a fence around it. Some would put one table here "for us" and another one over there "for them." Should we use one cup or many? Bread to be broken or bread already cut? Fermented wine or fresh grape juice? Sunday morning or some other time? Once a week or quarterly? Only local congregational members or all Christians present? Real body or only spiritual emblem? Only one element for all, or both for all? Approach the table or pass the emblems?

Some of those controversies are settled quite firmly in scriptural precedent and dictum. Some are petty matters of opinion. But none should divide Christians into warring factions.

This table is both a sign and a rallying point for our unity—unity of faith and submission, unity of thought and action, unity of grief and rejoicing. Here we act in unity. For we are one in Christ whose table it is.

PRAYER: Forgive us, God who is one, when we divide ourselves and oppose one another. Help us, Father, by this table to make ourselves one as You, the Son, and the Spirit are one.

THIS TABLE
Is for Knights

Legends of King Arthur and his round table of knights fill British literature. Stories of their deeds of valor are widely told.

This table in front of us is the round table of the knights of Christ. As was told of King Arthur and his knights, this table is round, for we come as equals here, all subservient to the King. For the knights, there is no head nor foot to this table; everyone sits *by* the King.

Here we assemble to honor the King and to pledge our continuing allegiance to Him. Here we discuss the wishes of the King, noble wishes indeed, for a peaceful, happy kingdom. Here we make our battle plans in the war against the great dragon.

Now, King Arthur may be legend or not, but this round table was established by a King of history and eternity. It is His table, and we are here, summoned by His invitation and command. It is His table, and we are here to "raise our swords" and salute Him: "King of kings and Lord of lords!" It is His table, and we leave it to do His bidding—to live holy and chivalrous lives of service . . . to battle with every nerve and sinew the monster of sin.

We are the knights of Christ. And this, this is the Roundtable of our Lord and King!

PRAYER: For deeming us worthy of serving in Your army, we thank You, O high King of glory. For arming us for the life-and-death struggle against the great dragon, we lift our swords in honor and to Your majesty.

Has Happy Family Memories

When fifteen hundred children were asked in a recent survey, "What makes a happy family?" they responded commonly with a "what-we-do-together" answer. They made no mention of the type of house they live in. No list of stuff they must have. Backyard play together, making a birdhouse together, trips together, *doing* things together—that's what makes a happy family.

Here at this table we do one of those things together as a family that can create happy family memories: *eat* together. And there is none of that bitter baiting shown so often at television family tables. Have you noticed that almost every time a family sits down to eat on television, someone is so mad at someone (or everyone) else, the meal is ruined? On many such occasions, one or more players angrily push back their chairs and stomp out, muttering those final vitriolic words guaranteed to increase the stock prices of every leading antacid manufacturer and to fill the appointment books of weary family counselors.

No such ill feelings come to this table. We do not carry our gripes about the Father's restrictions here; we know the restrictions are freeing, not limiting. There are no grumblings about the special treatment of the Elder Brother here. The family sits together here making happy memories. The children respect and honor the Father. The Father delights in His children. The siblings admire and defer to the First Son. The First Son smiles a blessing on each brother and sister present. Here, at this table, we are making happy family memories.

PRAYER: Father of us all, we are happy here at the family table. Allow us to capture the memories . . . for the week . . . for the years to come. All glory to You and the First Son.

Is the End

This table is an end table. Like end tables in the living room, it is a place to set things. But it is an end table in other, more significant ways as well.

This table represents the end of Jesus' ministry in the flesh, His death on the Jerusalem cross. There He finished the redemptive act for which He came. There He put an end to Satan's claim on the human race. There He could say, "It is finished." In one real sense, the sign on the cross could have correctly said, "The End."

Further, this table is an end table because it anticipates "the end," the end of time, the end of the material universe. For this table will be set until the very end . . . till Jesus steps onto that cloud that will carry Him from eternity to this time and place. And He will carry the label, "Omega—The End!"

Consider this table our study in eschatology—here we ponder the end things. Temporal existence is coming to an end. When the trumpet blows, announcing His coming, all will be able to sing the lyrics to the "Ta-Da!"—"The End." But thanks be to the God who knows the beginning from the end, Christ has put an end to the penalty for sin. And here at this end table, we have come to celebrate.

PRAYER: Alpha and Omega, we come as those limited by time; but we understand beginnings and endings. Thank You for this table that encourages us to consider the end, the end of the curse of sin, the end of all when Jesus comes.

THIS TABLE
Stirs Imagination

Many small children like to play under tables. Do you have some of those marvelous images of a preschooler hiding there, moving chairs as doors, pulling dish cloths to curtain imaginary windows? Imagination and a good table can provide hours of serious fun.

Does this table of the Lord stir your imagination? Do you ever see yourself at Calvary? Are you up close, wide-eyed? Or are you cowering at the back of the crowd? Are you friend or foe there? Are you, perhaps, *behind* the cross, so that your eyes never meet Jesus' eyes? Or do you catch yourself pulling one of those "dish-cloth curtains" across, to hide yourself from Him . . . to keep Him from seeing into the home of your soul? Have you ever heard, in your mind's ear, those hammer blows, "kathunk!" of nail through flesh and into wood? Ever heard the two thieves cursing

Rome, Jerusalem, soldiers, bystanders, God—everything that moves and everything that doesn't? How vivid is your imagination, here at this table where the children of God assemble for serious re-creation?

This is a table that must stir your imagination. Not of things fanciful. Not of play. But of reality. And of life and death. Pull the "chair" aside; crawl under the cross today. But do not attempt to hide from the Savior. Look Him straight in the eye and say, "I'm sorry, Lord." Then revel in His smile that He returns . . . here at His table under which we assemble for worship.

PRAYER: In the name of our friend Jesus, we come into Your house, O God. We have come to sit beneath His cross . . . where He has re-created us so that we can be His friends. Thank You for the images stirred up for us here.

Has No Surprises

When we approach tables, occasionally we get surprises. Did your mother—or father—ever set a dish on the table and say, "Surprise!"? Did you ever take that first bite of a tantalizing and attractive casserole and wide-eyedly think, "Surprise!"?

This table before us is a table of no surprises. We know what is here. It is dependably predictable. On this table we find the loaf—a simple piece of unleavened bread that hearkens back to the hurried and pure bread of the Old Testament Passover and to the pure bread of the body of Christ. On this table we find the cup filled with the juice of the grape—an appropriate representation of the One who likened himself to the vine, the One whose own blood flowed to create and sustain life. He said profoundly, "These simple emblems are my body and blood."

Of course, there is something about

this table that *is* surprising. No one could have anticipated God's designing it. Wonder and astonishment are natural here. This is the table of the unexpected gift, as if God were jumping out of the dark and yelling, "Surprise!" and filling the space with His light. Of course, there is something surprising here. But there are still no surprises. You and I know God's gift; we know He gives unexpectedly and without reason . . . except for the fact that He loves us. "Surprise!" No surprise.

PRAYER: You have surprised us with salvation, God of the unexpected. You have proved yourself dependable and faithful, the God of no surprises. Help us to be so predictable in Christ. Help us to surprise others with the great good news.

Inspires Song

Grand songs have been written, played, and sung about this table. "Bread of Heaven, on Thee We Feed," and "Here, O My Lord, I See Thee Face to Face." Nothing surprising about such a phenomenon. Grand songs flow from deep emotions, and this is a time and place of deep emotion. Recall that after the Lord's Supper was first ordained, Jesus and His apostles sang a song—of joy, I imagine—before they left for those dark, sad hours in the garden of Gethsemane.

Obviously, we could here sing a dirge. Here we grieve because of the death of our Elder Brother. But we could sing an operetta here, for this is a table that makes our heart light—the burden of our sins lifted and removed. Perhaps we could sing a quartet number here, for we all sing different parts in different voices, but we want to make a beautiful harmony together. Could an opera be appropriate? Of course, for most operas are tales of great tragedy, as is the story at this table. Possibly, a symphony in the background would be the best choice, for a great theme repeated over and over and ending in a bright crescendo is certainly similar to what we do here.

This table and grand songs go together. There is great reason to sing. What is your grand song of redemption that you are singing? Sing it unto the Lord!

PRAYER: Our songs rise to You feebly, O God who hears, for our voices have been weakened by sin. Forgive our sins. Accept our songs. We sing them to You and to the Son.

Is Unforgettable

Those who have studied human memory have disproved certain old theories and confirmed others. The mind is not a muscle, as some early thought, but regular use does appear to enhance ability. And, not at all surprisingly, they have affirmed that repetition is a key factor in memory. This is why some of us still remember the combination of a locker or mailbox that long ago was part of our lives. We "overlearned" it, in the word of the psychologists, from years of daily use.

Visual symbols and mnemonics (ni-*mah*-nics) are other key elements. Some of us old-timers could still recognize Dick and Jane and Spot, images that elicit both positive and negative memories!

Here at the Lord's table, we have both of these important elements for memory. How could we forget the Lord's death, in all its shame and glory? Every week we focus our minds on His dying. Week after week we come back. Week after week after week we stop to remember Calvary and the old rugged cross. Repetition is important to remembering.

Also, the visual symbols here are at the heart of our recall. The loaf and the cup are, by God's intent, our seeable symbols. The one stirs us to consider the flesh of our Lord: He became flesh and dwelt among us. Flesh—mortal, human, capable of aging and dying. The other emblem causes us to ponder the blood of our Lord. Human blood coursed through His arteries and veins. Life-giving, nutritional, oxygen-bearing blood, capable of leaving the body at any point His skin was pierced.

God has made it easy for us to re-member. He gives us both repetition and visual symbol. How could we forget the death of our Lord? How could we?

PRAYER: Creator of mind and memory, we praise You for the wisdom You have shown in helping us remember the death of Your Son.

Is Not Commonplace

Some events are ordinary, commonplace. The Tupperware Corporation says that somewhere in the world a Tupperware party begins every 2.7 seconds. Every day one hundred million or more times someone pulls out a dollar (or a drachma!) to purchase a lottery ticket. Hardly any jurisdiction that has instituted a 911 service can keep up with the emergency calls—real and imagined. Throughout the day, all over the earth, forty-four thousand thunderstorms vent their short-lived rage. Yes, some things are ordinary, commonplace.

But gathering at this table is extraordinary . . . special. Here we come but once a week. Here we must have more enthusiasm than a Tupperware host. Much, much, much more hope than a lottery ticket buyer. More sense of urgency than an emergency medical technician.

More sense of awe than is generated by a day's worth of lightning and thunder. Enthusiasm, hope, urgency, awe—this table can elicit them all. But we must consider its practical, day-to-day value, the anticipation it represents, the life-and-death nature of its subject matter, the overwhelming presence of God that is implied and promised.

Some events are ordinary, commonplace. This one is not. Can you work up the enthusiasm, the hope, the urgency, the awe? Can it become extraordinary, special to you?

PRAYER: God of the extraordinary, we bow humbly in Your presence, for we are ordinary and small. Thank You for bringing the extraordinary into our lives. Thank You for the special time and special place we now occupy.

Evokes Memories of Egypt

Do you remember your days in Egypt? No, not that Egypt; most of us have never been there. Do you remember your days in the Egypt of your bondage to sin? It is hot and oppressive there. Little joy was found there. Oh, an occasional smile came, such as at the birth of a child. But soon the sad realization struck you that the child was also born into slavery and had no real future of peace, comfort, happiness. Egypt was only a place to escape.

And one day most of us chose to leave Egypt. Convinced that God knew the way and would lead us, we committed ourselves to Him. We passed through the waters of the Red Sea and there separated ourselves from the oppression of sin—left it behind, "in the wash!"

This is a table designed to stir memories of Egypt. Memories of the hard life of sin. Memories of the Red Sea of baptism where we went into the water pursued by sin but came out, leaving sin behind, "dead in the water!" Here we have memory of that great demonstration of the power of God—one redemptive act. Before this table, we were in Egypt, in bitter bondage. After this table, we are on the way to the promised land. The Way leads there . . . there to the place where He has prepared a place for us, in one of those mansions He has erected in His death and unlocked in His resurrection. Here at this table, week to week, we say good-bye to Egypt. Good-bye!

PRAYER: We thank You, God of Moses, for those revealing stories of the Old Testament. Thank You for picturing our rescue from the Egypt of sin. And thank You for the reality of our rescue in Christ's death.

THIS TABLE
Is for Conversation

Tables lend themselves to conversation. The personal and intimate distance of the table—an arm's reach away—lends itself to personal, intimate conversation. That grand image in the Sistine Chapel of God's finger just a tiny gap from man's finger is the same image as at this table. God sits an arm's length away; He can be touched here.

And at this table He has spoken: "This is my beloved Son. Hear Him." And the Son sitting at His right hand has spoken— from the cross: "It is finished! My body and my blood are given for you." Now we must speak here, by our deed: "He is Lord! I do this because You say to, Lord. I do this because I want to obey You."

But our conversation is not only submissive, but active and full of joy. "Thank You, Father, for sending Bread from Heaven. Thank You, Jesus, for breaking the

Bread for us and filling our cups to over-flowing."

At tables we talk of business, of problems of the world, of delights in our days. There is no subject we cannot broach here with the Father and the Son. Here we must share both our sorrows and our happiness with God. He is sharing here both His sorrow and His happiness with us. Personal, intimate words. For that is what a table lends itself to.

PRAYER: We have come to talk to You here, O Father. We have come in the name of Your Son. Thank You for sharing sorrows and joys with us. Help us to share the same with You at this personal, intimate table.

Under or On
THIS TABLE

"Under the table" is an expression for crooked dealings. It indicates a secret, sinful transaction. Invisible. Done in the dark, lest the light shrivel it into the ugly thing that it is.

"On the table" is an expression for open, honest dealings. It indicates a deed is overt and righteous. Fully visible. Done in the light so that the light can magnify the beautiful thing that it is.

Nothing at this Lord's table is "under the table." Everything is "on the table." God has laid out on the table the elements of His deed, His overt and righteous deed. The crucifixion of His Son was fully visible, set in a public place . . . on a hill . . . just outside the capital city . . . right along a well-traveled highway. It was in the light of day . . . until God *had* to draw a curtain of darkness over the ugliness of sin, lest that sin overwhelm the goodness of the deed.

The deed was witnessed by many, some of whom have described it graphically for us.

We do not come here to deal with the Lord "under the table." We have no secrets from Him here, and there is absolutely nothing evil or underhanded here. This is a table of pure righteousness, His righteousness. Our sins *and* our faith must be "on the table," open to His omnipotent eye. We must be transparent to Him here, for He has made the death of His Son visible to us . . . here . . . "on the table."

PRAYER: God of openness, may we be as open to You as You are to us. We praise You that Christ's sacrifice was openly seen, to His great shame but to our great glory.

At Christmastime

Though we do not usually associate this table with Christmas, it is easy to do so. Christmas and this table both celebrate the incarnation. The image we have of the newborn cradled in the manger, and the image seen in the bread of this table are one and the same: God became flesh. He was infant, child, teenager, adult; He became one of us. Both the manger and the emblems of this table are reminders of that holy truth.

Christmas is noted as a time of giving, and so is this table. In both cases, God is the benefactor and we are the glad recipients. Christmas tells us He gave up the glory and honor of Heaven to be a lowly servant among us. This table tells us He gave up His lifeblood to cover our sins.

Christmas is both a solemn and a festive time, and so is this table. There is solemnity at the manger because we worship the Christ child in quiet and holiness, and solemnity at this table because we worship the adult Christ giving himself willingly for our evil. We are festive at the manger because we want to join the angels' jubilation, and festive at this table because we want to laugh with joy at our personal salvation.

Christmas is special, a once-a-year occasion, and this table is special, a once-a-week event. We must approach each with that "this-is-special" attitude. This table we should approach with all the anticipation with which a child approaches Christmas, all the sparkle in the eye, all the anxious focus.

Incarnation. Giving. Solemn. Festive. Special. The words can be used for both these holy times: Christmas and the Lord's table. Both are opportunities for our sincere, heartfelt worship.

PRAYER: For the stories of the real events of Christmas and Calvary, we praise your name, O God of both. Give us the spirit of worship for each.